Contents

Air is important

How often do you think about the air around you? For most people, the answer is never. Yet air is very important to us: we simply can't live without it. That's because air contains a **gas** called **oxygen** that all animals need to survive.

Air is all around us. We can't see, smell, or taste the air but we need it to survive.

When we ▶ breathe, we suck air into our **lungs**. That's how oxygen gets inside our bodies.

Many animals ▶ breathe in air. They need oxygen just like us.

Dirty air

In wild, empty parts of the world, the air is very clean. But in places where there are millions of people, the air is often dirty. That's because people burn **fuels** that **pollute** the air. Polluted air is bad for us and can harm our lungs.

The smoke from this bonfire comes from burning wood. Burning fuel pollutes the air with dirt and harmful gases.

Air pollution can make ▶
breathing difficult. In some
people it may cause **asthma**.

What is asthma?
Asthma is a kind of **allergy**.
It makes people cough, wheeze
and feel short of breath.

▲ **Antarctica** is so cold that no one lives there.
That's why the air here is very clean.

Too much traffic

There are millions of cars and trucks on our roads, and they all need petrol to move. Petrol is a fuel. When it is burned inside an engine, it makes dirty, smelly **fumes**. These puff out of the exhaust pipe and pollute the clean, fresh air.

Every year there are more and more cars on our roads. This is bad for the **environment**.

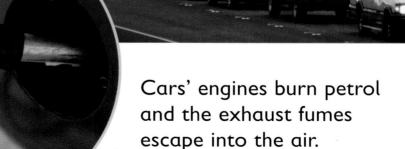

Cars' engines burn petrol and the exhaust fumes escape into the air.

◄ Car fumes contain gases that pollute the air. We breathe them in as we walk along the street.

People with asthma ▶ have to take a special medicine, which they breathe into their lungs. Air pollution makes asthma worse.

Going to school

Millions of people use a car to get around. Many children travel to school by car. What does this do to the streets around the school? What does this do to the air? Look at the picture to see the problems.

Each car is carrying just one or two children.

The cars are blocking the road. This is dangerous for people on foot, who have to squeeze between them.

The cars have made a traffic jam. Now none of them can move.

All the cars are burning petrol.

The car fumes pollute the air.

Breathing polluted air harms us all – particularly people with asthma.

A better way to school

There are many ways of getting to school each morning without using the car. You can see some of these in the picture below. What has happened to the streets around the school? What do you think has happened to the air?

The school bus is carrying lots of children. This is a good use of fuel.

These children are sharing a lift to school.

There are fewer cars on the road so the air is cleaner and nicer to breathe.

Some children are cycling to school with an adult. There are cycle lanes on the road.

Some children are walking to school with an adult.

Older children walk to school in a group.

Cutting down on traffic

Leaving our cars at home now and then will help us to burn less fuel. It's good to take **public transport** when we can, such as buses, trams and trains. Bikes are another way of getting around, and give us some exercise, too!

Many city buses and trams move faster than cars because they have their own special lanes.

▲ Trains carry hundreds of passengers. They make good use of fuel.

◄ Bikes are a great way of getting around. They are cheap, clean and easy to park.

Making energy

It's not just traffic that pollutes the air — **power stations** do, too. Power stations make **electricity**. Most of them do this by burning huge amounts of fuel, such as oil, gas or coal. This makes fumes that pollute the air.

This power station burns coal to make its electricity. Other power stations use gas or oil.

What would we do without electricity? It provides energy for street lights, cinemas, trains, trams and many other useful things.

Using energy at home

Power stations burn fuel to make electricity. This provides us with energy to use in the home. But take a good look at the house in the picture. Is the energy being used wisely?

The oven is almost empty. It is heating up a meal for one.

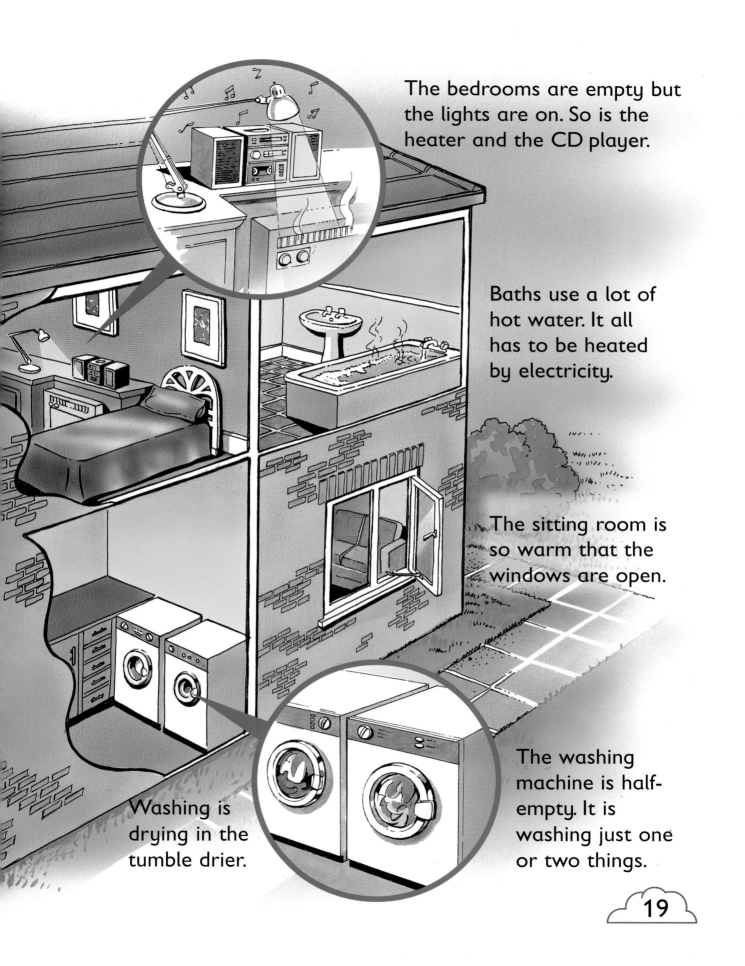

The bedrooms are empty but the lights are on. So is the heater and the CD player.

Baths use a lot of hot water. It all has to be heated by electricity.

The sitting room is so warm that the windows are open.

Washing is drying in the tumble drier.

The washing machine is half-empty. It is washing just one or two things.

19

A better way with energy

We can't stop using electricity but we can try to use it more wisely. Look at the house in the picture. Can you see how energy is being saved? Savings like this can help cut pollution. If we use less electricity, power stations will burn less fuel.

A microwave oven uses less electricity and heats up food very fast.

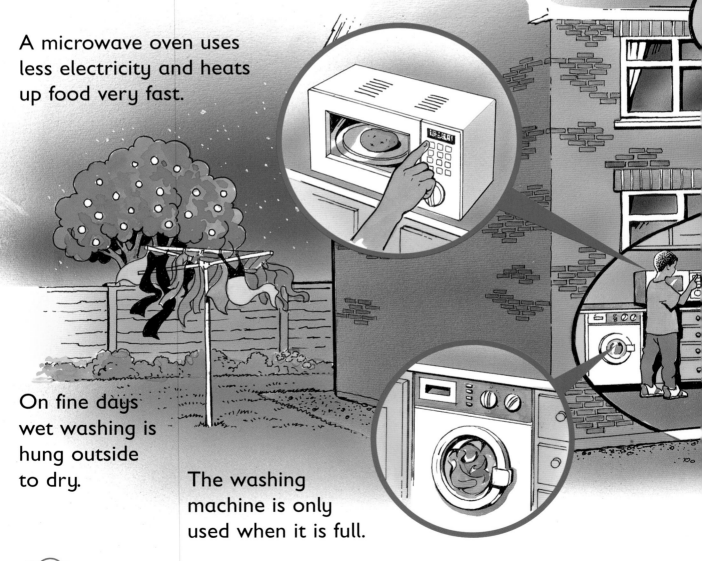

On fine days wet washing is hung outside to dry.

The washing machine is only used when it is full.

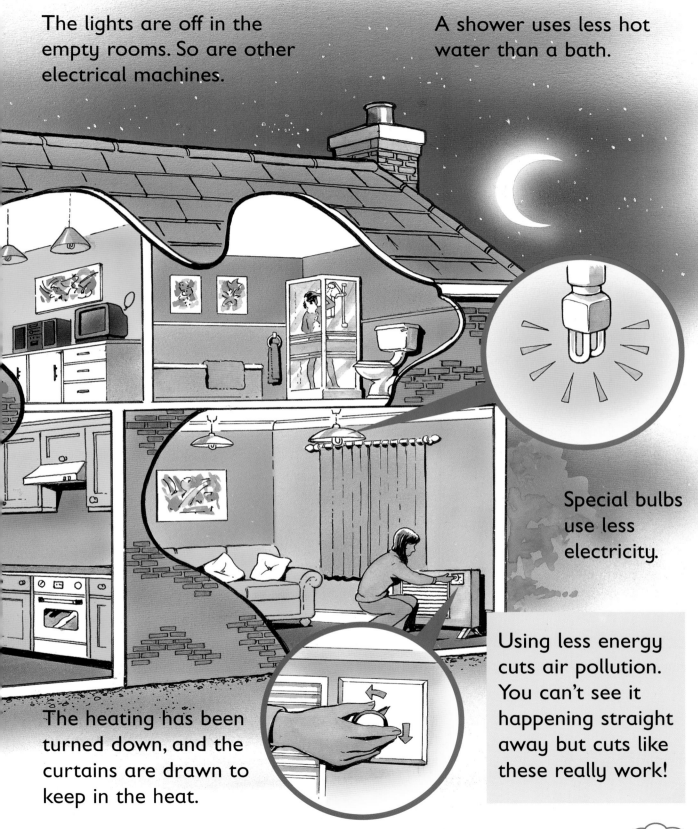

The lights are off in the empty rooms. So are other electrical machines.

A shower uses less hot water than a bath.

Special bulbs use less electricity.

Using less energy cuts air pollution. You can't see it happening straight away but cuts like these really work!

The heating has been turned down, and the curtains are drawn to keep in the heat.

Cleaner energy

There are other ways of making electricity besides burning fuels. Electricity can be made from the Sun, the wind and flowing water. These kinds of energy are **natural** and clean. They do not produce dirty fumes.

▲ Many pocket calculators run on solar power.

▲ Electricity made from the Sun is called **solar power**. This emergency phone collects sunlight in **solar cells**, which change it into electricity.

◄ A **wind turbine** uses the power of the wind to make electricity. Inside each turbine a special machine is powered by the spinning blades.

Inside this dam there are ▶ huge wheels that are turned by the rushing water. They drive machines that make electricity.

Recycling saves energy

It takes huge amounts of energy to collect a **raw material** and turn it into something else – for example, to cut down trees and turn them into paper. A lot of energy can be saved by **recycling** old materials such as paper, metal and glass.

It takes more energy to make paper from trees than from recycled paper.

Glass bottles and metal cans are easy to recycle. Recycling them uses less energy than making them from raw materials.

PLEASE RECYCLE

Buy recycled goods whenever you can. They take less energy to produce.

Small actions, big results

Is it possible for you to fight air pollution? Of course, it is! If your small steps are copied by millions of people, the results for the Earth will be huge! Everyone on Earth shares the planet. Everyone can help to save it.

What would happen if everyone used public transport?

There would be fewer cars burning fuel. The air would be cleaner and nicer to breathe.

What would happen if everyone used electricity wisely?

The country would need less electricity. Some power stations could be shut down.

What would happen if we all recycled our rubbish?

GREEN
BOTTLES & JARS
ONLY
NO PYREX OR CROCKERY PLEASE

Many factories would use less energy. This would cut the air pollution that comes from burning fuel.

Over to you!

No one wants to choke on dirty fumes. Why not try one of the ideas below, and help to clean up the air?

Make posters to encourage people to walk, cycle or use public transport. Put them up in your school, local library, club house or home.

Keep a diary of the number of times in a week your family uses the car. Perhaps your parents could save fuel by combining several short journeys into a longer trip.

Suggest that everyone in the family has a bike. There are plenty of second-hand ones around.

Are there bus lanes and cycle lanes in your town? If not, write to your local paper to suggest the idea.

Do a survey to find out how people in your class come to school in the morning. Perhaps some of you could walk together or share a lift?

Recycle as much rubbish as you can. Suggest that your house has different bins to sort paper, glass, plastics and cans.

Talk to your parents about how you could save electricity at home. Look back at the ideas on pages 20-21.

Put up notes around your home to remind people to turn off lights and electric machines.

Save electricity by fitting energy-saving light bulbs.

Join a group that helps to protect the environment. Some of the groups you could try are:

Friends of the Earth *www.foe.co.uk*
Greenpeace *www.greenpeace.org.uk*

Glossary

Allergy An allergy makes the body react badly to something that may not harm other people. Air pollution and certain foods are two things that can cause allergies.

Antarctica The frozen land around the South Pole, where the weather is always very cold.

Asthma An allergy that makes breathing difficult.

Electricity A kind of energy that provides us with heat, light and the power to run machines.

Energy The power that makes machines and living things able to work. We can get energy from fuels, sunlight, water and wind.

Environment The land, air and sea that make the world around us.

Fuel Wood, coal, oil or some other material that can be burned to produce heat and power.

Fumes The mixture of dirt and gases that is made by burning fuel.

Gas A substance like air, which is not solid or liquid. Air is made of a mixture of different gases.

Lungs The parts in a human's and animal's body that help to take in oxygen from the air.

Natural Found in the world around us.

Oxygen A gas that is found in the air, and which all animals need to survive.

Pollute To spoil the air, land or water with harmful substances.

Power station A large building where electricity is made.

Public transport Buses, trains and other vehicles that carry fare-paying passengers.

Raw materials Natural materials that are used to make something new.

Recycle To take a material, such as old paper, and use it again to make something new.

Solar cell A small device that makes electricity from sunlight.

Solar power Electricity made from the Sun's heat and light.

Wind turbine A machine that uses the power of the wind to make electricity.

Index